FOREWORD

MOTHER MARY CLARE has for many years contributed to a variety of courses for Religious held at Spode House. Several of these contributions have already appeared among the Fairacres Publications, revealing the deep experience the author has brought to these conferences and the great value of what she came to give. The printed word cannot, of course, convey all the power of the message Mother Mary Clare has shared over the years with so many Religious; nevertheless the substance of what she has had to say can be read with considerable benefit.

These talks have also a particular value by reason of their context. For the conferences addressed by Mother Mary Clare were gatherings of Roman Catholic Religious, men and women, and in this respect the papers have had considerable ecumenical importance. This does not consist only in the fact that a wise and widely-experienced Religious from the Church of England came to teach a group of Roman Catholic Religious about the doctrines of her Church. They have a wider significance.

Ecumenical dialogue for some time consisted of the exchange of views—two communities living on adjacent islands, shouting to each other across the water and exchanging information about their respective islands, the geography, the climate, etc. Discussion and information are of course necessary in order that differing groups should get to know each other. This is the first approach to unity, but it would be a mistake to regard as some sort of achievement what is no more than a preparation. Without really knowing one another, a young couple meet and fall in love. For a time they face each other as separate entities, each drawing out and discovering the other's personality. Then comes the moment when they no longer face each other, but stand together before the altar both facing God as two persons seeking their union and their fulfilment through him. This is a stage which a number of Anglicans and Catholics are approaching—seeking the one truth together—facing God rather than each other. Both bring the fruits of a long and separate tradition, and the combination of the two yields fresh insights into the truth.

The first stage of ecumenism, then, is the meeting of members of separated Churches in the love of friendship, desiring unity but conscious of their differences and eager to discuss them. The next stage is one in which differences are forgotten in the awareness of the unutterable truth

1

and love of God which all are seeking together. In this quest the Christian, and particularly the Religious, is ready to learn from any spiritual master who follows the Lord and Master who alone 'has the words of eternal life'. The particular Church from which the teacher comes is irrelevant; such differences are forgotten in the urgent desire to approach the face of God together.

Such an approach to truth and love is developing in many quarters; groups of Roman Catholic and Anglican theologians meeting, officially and unofficially in all kinds of different circumstances, are making their contribution without any sense of belonging to different sides, but, each with his own approach and special field of study, searching the Scriptures together. It would seem at this point that the awkward word 'ecumenism', with its undertones of 'separated brethren', could be dropped in favour of some other phrase which would give the sense of a certain unity achieved, of the live seed sown and sprouting.

The talks by Mother Mary Clare are not only a splendid example of the way in which this unity is already growing—groups of Catholic Religious listening intently to an Anglican Superior—but their actual subject provides the basis of this unity. Listening together to God and to one another is the secret of growth in it. An open mind as well as an open heart has a freshness about it that is redolent of the Church in her beginnings. Since those beginnings minds have tended to become closed to one another and therefore closed also to God. In the more recent past these mental barriers have begun to yield to the strong breath of the Spirit. Therein lies our hope of unity.

Here in this place much of our listening has come about through the work of Mother Mary Clare. And so I take this opportunity of expressing the gratitude of all at Spode House, and of the many Religious who have listened to her under its roof. Our Lord will surely reward her by showing her the increase in his Church of that unity which she has so much at heart.

CONRAD PEPLER O.P.
Warden of Spode House
Hawksyard

LISTENING TO GOD AND LISTENING TO COMMUNITY

I

WHEN FATHER CONRAD first sent me the proposed title of my talks I thought, rather naively, that the subject would divide neatly into two papers: in the morning 'Listening to God' and in the afternoon 'Listening to Community'.

On further reflection it became very obvious that in the Christian context of the Religious Life, which we are all trying to explore, it is no more possible to separate listening to God and listening to Community than it is to separate the two commandments to love God and to love one's neighbour. Loving God must overflow into love of neighbour; and to love one's neighbour without loving God would be an exercise in humanism which need not necessarily lead to any profound knowledge and understanding of the depths of God's love. I therefore propose to consider this subject as a whole, to try to explore what listening really means both in relation to God and to Community. I will begin with a quotation from Thomas Merton:

> 'Tell me,' said Yen Hui, 'what is fasting of the heart?'
> Confucius replied: 'The goal of fasting is inner unity. This means hearing, but not with the ear; hearing, but not with the understanding; hearing with the spirit, with your whole being. The hearing that is only in the ears is one thing. The hearing of the understanding is another. But the hearing of the spirit is not limited to any one faculty, to the ear, or to the mind. Hence it demands the emptiness of all the faculties. And when the faculties are empty, then the whole being listens. There is then a direct grasp of what is right there before you that can never be heard with the ear or understood with the mind. Fasting of the heart empties the faculties, frees you from limitation and from preoccupation. Fasting of the heart begets unity and freedom.'

> *The Way of Chuang Tzu*, p.52

3

The most difficult and most decisive part of prayer is acquiring the ability to listen. To listen, according to the dictionary, is 'attentively to exercise the sense of hearing'. It is not a passive affair, a space when we don't happen to be doing or saying anything and are, therefore, automatically able to listen. It is a conscious, willed action, requiring alertness and vigilance, by which our whole attention is focussed and controlled. So it is difficult. And it is decisive because it is the beginning of our entry into a personal relationship with God in which we gradually learn to let go of ourselves and allow the Word of God to speak within us.

I am glad the subject is *listening* and not *silence* or *stillness* because I want to avoid the negative overtones that can be attached to silence. Silence is a word much used in the present-day search for simpler contemplative prayer, but one that is potentially dangerous for the seekers. And, indeed, for Religious who are committed to the apostolic ministry—as so many are. On the other hand, it is they who might be tempted to think or to say that, because of their involvement in a noisy world, silence is not only impossible but irrelevant.

There is a silence which is merely pointless and negative. There is a silence which harms others by its coldness and self-absorption. The silence of the totally self-centred person is a terrible and destructive thing. Nor is silence in itself an ultimate good. In one of his sermons the great Anglican divine John Donne describes heaven as the place where there 'shall be no noise nor silence but one equall music . . .' Silence is a beginning, a way by which we learn the positive and difficult art of listening, of using not only our ears but our whole selves in order to attend: '. . . hearing, but not with the ear; hearing, but not with the understanding; hearing with the spirit, with your whole being.'

OBSTACLES TO LISTENING

Being the activist people that we naturally are—and who among us could claim to be a good listener all the time?—it would be worth our while to think for a moment about some of the obstacles to positive and creative listening.

Is it not the case that much of our time is spent in talking and listening to ourselves? So, our own voice is the chief obstacle in the way of listening either to God or to other people. We chatter away to others in the attempt to make contact with them, to impress them, to amuse or instruct them, or even to relieve ourselves. We do an immense amount of sheer talking in any ordinary day. Speech, after all, is one of the chief means by which society functions.

When we are not talking to others we are often talking to God. 'Listen to me God', we say, and we explain to Him about ourselves, our neighbours, our needs, hopes and fears, bombarding him with information and requests. And, of course, when we are not talking to others or to God we are probably carrying on a continuous dialogue with ourselves that goes on and on, blocking our ears to anything else and monopolising our whole attention.

One moment of willed listening when we are alone shows us how much we are missing even of ordinary sounds. If we take our minds off ourselves for a moment we may hear a bird singing, a bell in the distance, the gentle rustle of the wind in the leaves, the murmur of the tide as it ebbs and flows over the pebbles on the beach, even our own breathing; but generally we drown such sounds with our interior chatter. It is not external noise, primarily, but self-preoccupation that prevents us from listening.

It is often said that our world is so full of noise we can't listen any longer. But is not this just an excuse? If we could escape from traffic, jet planes, radio, TV, and all the ordinary noises of civilization on to a lonely mountain (as I have so often done in North Wales where there are only the birds and a few sheep), we might still find it hard to listen. The external noises of the world are as nothing compared to the din we make within ourselves. We can be deaf to the loudest noise as long as our own inner self remains unstilled. Only later on do external noises become a distraction.

HOW ARE WE TO BECOME PEOPLE WHO LISTEN?

So often in our personal encounters with God or with other people we can echo that line of Eliot's in *The Dry Salvages*: 'We had the experience but missed the meaning.' It is we who need to stop talking to God, to others and to ourselves and learn instead to listen to the Word of God speaking silently in our hearts. It is a lifelong task.

First of all we must be humble enough to know we are noisy. The ability to tell oneself to be quiet, to stop talking, to 'shut up', is not easily acquired. We need to be aware that we are not ready for stillness.

> I said to my soul, be still and wait without hope
> For hope would be hope for the wrong thing; wait without love,
> For love would be love of the wrong thing; there is yet faith,

But the faith and the hope and the love are all in the waiting.
Wait without thought for you are not ready for thought:
So the darkness shall be light and the stillness the dancing.

East Coker, T. S. Eliot

Secondly, we need to *practise focussing our attention*. Probably most of us find that when we are listening to a piece of music, for example, our attention soon slips. The same is true of prayer; listening to God through the Divine Office, through the Liturgy, through the Scriptures, is not automatic. We need to practise it and to set aside a definite time in order, as Metropolitan Antony Bloom puts it, 'just to sit before the Face of God'.

There is a whole asceticism of listening to be learned. It needs a conscious and controlled effort to become still and attentive and to let others speak to us as themselves. It is the slow and painful process of constantly recalling our attention to the matter in hand, whether it be a person, a book, or perhaps the tools we handle. One help towards acquiring this art is to take a word or a phrase or a short passage of Scripture and give it our whole attention, resisting the desire to go on reading or to look up some related fact, but instead just letting it speak to us until it begins to sing its own song within us. It is then, as you know, that we are on the threshold of prayer. There are, of course, moments when our whole attention is caught and our whole being focussed on God with an awareness of immense need or perhaps of overwhelming delight. But in ninety-nine per cent of our moments we have no such experience—what is required of us is diligence.

POINTS FOR CONSIDERATION

'We had the experience but missed the meaning.' Here are a few points around which we might gather our thoughts and prayer.

1) We need to empty ourselves of our preconceptions, prejudices and reservations, not only about the person to whom we are listening but also about the matter of which he or she may be talking. We shall do this successfully only if we see listening to others as an extension and, indeed, as a fruit of our listening to God.

2) We need to bring to this listening the same positive determination with which we find time each day for God in order to make a space for Him in our lives, space to quieten our frustrated world-worn spirits, space for listening, space to rest in a dimension in which time has entered into eternity and eternity into time. We say so often and so unthinkingly,

'There is no time, I have no time', yet there is all the time in the world if we are listening to God the Holy Spirit within us.

3) I suggest we ask ourselves, what do we hope or expect or fear when we try to listen to community? In listening to God how do we receive his invitation to a deeper response? Or when we listen to others, do we open ourselves to what they have to say, or do we react to it with the impulse of the moment, whatever it may be—an arbitrary decision, perhaps, or hostility, conciliation or even neutrality? What, in fact, do we hear?

'Human kind', says Eliot, 'cannot bear very much reality.' Is it reality we fear as we try to empty our souls before God on the one hand, or when we find ourselves cut off from people by our preconceived ideas and opinions about them on the other? The God of *The Hound of Heaven*, or the God of some tormented angry 'client' who has arrived at a Samaritan Centre, or perhaps at one of our convents, may easily be too much of a 'reality' for many of us. A first, tentative step, then, in the development of our ability to listen is to suspend our judgement and make a deliberate and disciplined attempt to become as really and truly 'open' as we should like to be, with all our hearts even more than with our minds; open to meet God where we are and therefore where he expects to find us (which will not necessarily be in St Teresa's Seventh Mansion!). We need to meet other people not where we think they are but where, perhaps, they know they are.

Finally, in this first part of my paper, there is another aspect of listening I would like to touch on, even if it takes our thoughts rather beyond the scope of what was originally intended.

In Henri Nouwen's most recently published book called *Reaching Out*, 'The three movements of the spiritual life', the author suggests three levels of awareness on which a practical plan for living one's life in the power of the Spirit may be based in order to lead us to our ultimate goal—union with God. Father Nouwen proposes firstly, a movement from loneliness to solitude, which is reaching out to the deepest centre of our being; secondly, a reaching out to our fellow human beings; and thirdly, reaching out to God in prayer. Now these three movements all require on our part a willingness to listen—to ourselves, to community, to God. It is by listening that we become aware of our own nothingness without God, and—especially important for our present consideration—it is by listening with a growing sense of the coinherence of human lives that we avoid self-righteousness and are enabled to grow in compassion.

I suggest therefore that as a link between the general consideration of our subject and its more practical application in the second half of my paper, we should think of listening as a means of growing in compassionate solidarity. In the words of Henri Nouwen:

> The movement from loneliness to solitude . . . is not a movement of a growing withdrawal from, but rather a movement towards, a deeper engagement in the burning issues of our time. The movement from loneliness to solitude is a movement that allows us to perceive interruptions as occasions for a conversion of heart, which makes our responsibilities a vocation instead of a burden, and which creates the inner space where a compassionate solidarity with our fellow human beings becomes possible. The movement from loneliness to solitude is a movement by which we reach out to our innermost being to find there our great healing powers, not as a unique property to be defended but as a gift to be shared with all human beings. And so, the movement from loneliness to solitude leads us spontaneously to the movement from hostility to hospitality. It is this second movement that can encourage us to reach out creatively to the many whom we meet on our way.
>
> (op. cit. p. 60. Published by Collins, 1976)

But first we must listen to others in order to be able to meet them where they are and so help them and be helped by them on the path of our mutual pilgrimage.

II

I HOPE THAT PRAYING and thinking together about listening to God and listening to community may have helped us to see that community—in whatever context we may use that word—asks of us a closer identification with each other as persons who have learned to listen with sensitivity and mutual compassion. Surely that is the real meaning of community. And I would like to add here something more specifically about community with special relevance for those who, in their own community, hold office of one sort or another.

Our ability to make community depends on our readiness to listen to each other. It depends on a certain openness and receptivity. It depends very specially on being ready to listen to and learn things that are unexpected and new to our experience in the Religious Life. It means being ready to learn from frustrations as well as from happiness, from experiences that seem to be negative as well as from positive ones. It means being ready to question oneself and to re-examine one's past experience.

We all know how much we have learnt from the community, and most of the learning in the Religious Life—not only what concerns practical matters—goes on in the course of conversations between Sisters. Superiors are to a large extent by-standers, whether we like it or not. Usually we like it, though sometimes we are a bit apprehensive about just what plots are being hatched or just what private psychotherapies are being applied!

Yet whether we are teachers or learners we must be open to listen to each other. This is a continuous process for a Religious from the day of her admission until the final consummation in death. And we must be equally prepared to learn by listening to our fellow lay Christians.

One important element of this learning which must continue all through our lives is the discovery of the truth about ourselves through listening to God in prayer and through listening to others. What are our strengths and our weaknesses? How do we function in large or small groups? Do we take charge, or do we opt out? How do we exercise authority—or don't we?

Community life, above everything else, forces us to live at close quarters with others. We cannot easily escape from them nor they from us, and any attempt to do so will be obvious to all. We are confronted with the more as well as the less admirable features both of ourselves and of our neighbours and must learn to live with them. So we learn to be generous both towards our own peculiarities and those of others. This is an endless challenge to tolerance, magnanimity, open-hearted listening and compassion. We are challenged not only in our personal relationships but by all that we find imperfect in the institutions in which we live and in the methods of those who run them. Here too, there is great need to practise acceptance and understanding if we are not to condemn ourselves to misery in the institutional communities.

From the first, therefore, the interplay of relationship with God and each other requires that we cherish no illusions as to anyone's omnipotence or omniscience. We should face the fact that authority in community is sometimes exercised by more or less muddle-headed people who have surprisingly little control over the persons and events they ostensibly direct. If we can grasp this fact fairly early on in community life it will save us from much rage and disappointment in the years that lie ahead. At the same time, if we are really God-orientated, if we are really growing in openness and listening sensitivity to each other, then, within the apparent limits of our situation, we have a surprising amount of opportunity for freedom and joy in Christian relationship, as well as a tremendous responsibility for one another. But, in relation to our subject, it is well known that one of the greatest difficulties of leadership is to have to deal with people who will not accept the responsibility of their freedom because they have not learnt to build up habits of listening with sensitivity.

Little that I have said so far is peculiar to Christianity, but now we must remind ourselves that, as members of the Christian community, let alone a religious community, we are not primarily for each other but for God. Our eyes and ears should be fixed not on each other but on God as we go forward, a group of persons drawn together by the same voice that asks for the attention of each and all. 'Speak, Lord, for your servant hears', said the child Samuel when God called him by name. He was called, and he heard, listened and responded. In all our Religious life we should have the same movements of the Spirit operating in us. The basis of any religious community is not merely a common rule, a common way of life, or even shared experience, but the Divine call which is addressed both corporately and individually to all its members.

10

DISCERNMENT IN LISTENING

Seen in this wider context, listening and silence, as we thought earlier, can be equated with compassion and loving awareness of each other. We must beware of patronising others, of any sense of conferring a benefit on them, and instead recognise ourselves as very ineffectual human beings trying to respond in human terms to another human being, one who is no better or worse, no more complicated, neither more nor less intelligent, sensitive or aware than ourselves. Unless we can do this we had better give up the attempt and let that other person to whom we thought we had so much to give by listening, save his or her breath.

True listening obviously needs careful training, but silence and listening are not by themselves the whole story. When we have begun to learn to listen we will notice certain things. We will actually hear external sounds with our ears, the ticking of a clock, the radio next door, the distant rush of traffic, as well as the sounds of the birds and the wind in the trees; and it is at this point that we can begin to discriminate and make ourselves choose what we will hear. This will lead us on to desire more and more external silence to correspond with the growing inner alertness and attentiveness which is the prelude to stillness before God. The solitary place, the lonely shore, these may have a real place in our prayer. We have to be able to hear external sounds before we can with any reality choose among them and exclude those which are unnecessary to us.

Then we will notice that we have begun to listen to ourselves. We probably won't like what we hear, but once we have begun to be really still, and have stopped deluding ourselves with our own ideas and suggestions, there is a chance that we may hear within ourselves what we most deeply desire but may still be afraid to face. Here again we will now be in a position to exercise discernment about our inner promptings, and also to recognise how in community we may be tempted to use our activity as an escape route from that inner awareness of what God is trying to say to us.

And so we will hear God. To speak of 'hearing' God is of course to use a metaphor meaning that we are focussing our attention on God in order to hear what He is saying to us through all the channels open to us as Christians. The Spirit of God speaks to us through the Scriptures, through the Liturgy, through the circumstances of our life, and through other people. The Spirit broods over the waters of our chaos and out of that chaos He brings order.

Thus we will hear others. But now I must enter a caveat on my subject. Precisely because of its importance, listening to others has become something of an idol among us, especially in these days of 'horizontal leadership'. We must, we say, listen to others, hear what they are saying to us—and hear all of it. Psychology as well as religion urges us to do so. The humanities and the social sciences are as eager as theology to make us listen to others. And it is indeed vital. We must take very seriously the need to understand, that is, to *stand under the other*. For example, as we all now realise, it has been our great error in missionary work in the past that we have not been ready to listen to what the religions of the world are saying to us. The same is true in other spheres also. But while our perceptions must be alert and entirely focussed on what is being said to us, we should be warned against two things.

First, it is not an easy matter for any of us to recognise our true identity: in fact it is a lifelong exploration. We must therefore be sensitively attuned and must pray for discretion and patience as we listen to others so that together we and they can get to the heart of the matter.

Secondly, we must use discernment about *what* we listen to. There is a great danger in opening ourselves to hear *everything* a person wants to say to us at that moment. To begin with, can we really bear it? Sometimes we can't, and it is the sin of curiosity that makes us listen to what we can neither understand nor share. Moreover, the person concerned will almost inevitably at a later date regret having told us 'everything', either because we were inadequate or because they think we have betrayed them, or from fear, or shame. It is not always necessary to hear everything. There is a definite limit to how much we can profitably hear from the lips of another person on any one occasion.

ACTION FROM LISTENING

Sometimes more is required of us than just listening. It may be that as a result we must speak or act.

We must learn to be still and to listen with our whole attention, but that is not the end any more than silence is an end in itself. Take the supreme mystery of the silence of Mary before the coming of the Incarnate Son. At the Annunciation we see a human being who listened totally with her whole self, but that was not the end. Out of that listening she not only heard the call, she obeyed. God's Word spoke itself fully in her silence. There is also the silence of Mary at the foot of the cross. She was unable to add one whit to the total offering of her Son, but by her silent compassion and identification with his will, she is for us all and for the ages to come the perfect example of the human will uniting itself with the supreme offering of God's redemptive action. Here listening and action reach their human climax.

The one who truly listens is also the one who truly obeys. If we accept the very serious task of stilling ourselves in order to listen to God we may be required to take action, and the result may be as devastating as the result of our Lady's 'Yes'—which was as a sword piercing her heart.

Speech is, of course, the most obvious means of communication we have, yet in a Religious community, drawn together in response to the Holy Spirit, it is silence and listening which do more than anything to unite us to God and to each other. I need hardly say that it is not our activity which blocks the lines of communication between ourselves and God and between ourselves and community, but our egoism that gets in the way. It is here that listening silence can be a means of purification. Only a listening silence can lead to a stilling of the mind, a cessation of the ceaseless chatter to ourselves about the memories which surge up from the unconscious. The cleansing of the memory is that aspect of purgation which makes room for the work of listening—our part in the dialogue of prayer with God. We must remember that it is no good trying to beat the mind into a state of concentration or to hammer it into a particular shape. That is a sheer effort of will, and very different from waiting on the power of God to draw all the faculties into unity. It is the uprising of love in the heart, the desire to belong utterly to God that cleanses us, and in the course of this process it is for Him to deal with the stirrings of our natural being. It is only when a soul is wholly given to Christ to be formed by divine Charity that there is a complete quieting of self. Only in the willingness to be conformed to God's will can true silence be found.

Stillness of mind leads on to stillness of soul so that the soul may be the true mirror that reflects the light of God. It is in that silence of the soul that we are brought into true dialogue with God and with each other, into the silence of our corporateness. We are emptied of self through humility, when we realise our own nothingness, and through the practice of obedience whereby the self is given entirely to God in the community. There must be a silence of the mind in which all the faculties are waiting on God, in the dark if need be, in the knowledge that we can find nothing in ourselves. There must be a silence of soul in order that the Spirit may reign there. In all this we remember that the aim is to arrive at unity, aware-ness and mutual sensitivity.

In this context, therefore, silence is crucial for the task of listening. Only by the positive use of silence can we hope to build up a life of unceasing prayer and habitual dependence on God which, when all else fails, will enable us to sustain the offering of apostolic ministry—the offering, that is, of our lives to Him.

CONCLUSION

I would like to gather up these thoughts on listening to God and listening to community in some words of André Louf:

> Prayer cleanses people and things. It lays their deep centre bare, and in so doing prayer restores and heals the creation, sees it in the light of God and brings it back to him. That is why all prayer is related to *blessing* and it will normally overflow into eucharistic *thanksgiving*.
>
> Because by praying he has found deep within his heart his true self, the man of prayer may now perhaps be able to identify everything else. He has acquired a new way of looking at people and things. From within his own centre he reaches also to the centre of everything that comes in his direction. And again, he is more sensitive to the masks that others wear, to everything that hinders the world from being itself before God . . . he *sees through* the outward appearance of people and things. The veil of egoism is for him already lifted. He *perceives* it all. As Isaac the Syrian wrote, 'he beholds the flame of things.'

Teach Us To Pray, pp. 106f.

FAIRACRES PUBLICATIONS

Complete List

BY GILBERT SHAW

ALSO AVAILABLE FROM SLG PRESS

All titles listed above are obtainable—postage extra—from:
SLG PRESS, Convent of the Incarnation, Fairacres, Oxford OX4 1TB.

A discount of one third is allowed for quantity orders.
Orders to the value of £10 net and over will be sent carriage paid (UK only).
Postage costs are difficult to assess, and items may be temporarily out of print or
deleted from the list. We therefore prefer customers to pay on receipt of their
order, or by blank cheque.

'LISTENING TO GOD AND LISTENING TO COMMUNITY' was first read at a Conference for Catholic Superiors at Spode House in February 1977 and is the sixth of the papers delivered by Mother Mary Clare at that well-known Catholic Conference centre to be published by SLG Press since 1970. Of the earlier papers, *Learning to Pray*, *The Apostolate of Prayer* and *Encountering the Depths* continue to be among the most widely read of the Fairacres Publications. For this latest one Father Conrad Pepler O.P. has kindly written a Foreword. In it he says:

> The talks by Mother Mary Clare are not only a splendid example of the way in which . . . unity is already growing—groups of Catholic Religious listening intently to an Anglican Superior—but their actual subject provides the basis of this unity. Listening together to God and to one another is the secret of growth in it. An open mind as well as an open heart has a freshness about it that is redolent of the Church in her beginnings. Since those beginnings minds have tended to become closed to one another and therefore closed also to God. In the more recent past these mental barriers have begun to yield to the strong breath of the Spirit. Therein lies our hope of unity.

MOTHER MARY CLARE is the former Mother General of the Sisters of the Love of God, an Anglican contemplative community whose mother house is at Fairacres, Oxford.

SLG PRESS
CONVENT OF THE INCARNATION
FAIRACRES   OXFORD
0X4 1TB

ISBN 0 7283 0076 1
ISSN 0307-1405